ISBN: 979-8-9893766-0-5
First Edition: 2023

Illustrations: Anastasia Cartovenco. karminaart11@gmail.com

*Dedicated to Iris, Mandy, Katya, Laurel, Joaquin,
Lana, Wendy, and Kazzi,
who helped Misha on her big adventure.*

Acknowledgments

I'd like to express my deepest gratitude to everyone who made this book possible.

To my family and friends, thank you for your encouragement and enthusiasm.

To my talented illustrator, Anastasia, your beautiful artwork brought Misha's journey to life in a way that words alone could not. And thank you a million times for every else you did to help make this story into a book.

To Nathan and Mischa, who this story is all about - your incredible bond and enduring spirit inspired the heart of this tale.

A heartfelt thank you to the people online who shared the news of Misha when she was lost and to the people of Ukraine who provided inspiration through their resilience and compassion.

And to all the young readers and families who pick up this book, thank you for allowing "Misha's Big Adventure" to be a part of your lives.
May this story inspire your own adventures and the power of hope.

Misha's Big Adventure

by Jamila Williams
Illustrated by Anastasia Cartovenco

Misha was a sweet dog who lived
in a market in the city of Kyiv.
It was busy during in the day,
but lonely at night.

Misha didn't have a family, but she made many friends. Sometimes Babusya took Misha home at night so she didn't have to be alone.

One morning, the market closed down. Babusya
promised to help Misha find a forever home.

That is how Misha met Nathan who invited Misha
to live with him. And he gave the best scratches!

8

Misha was so happy. She loved her new home.
She had a special bed and her own bowl.
She hung out with Nathan all day,
in the house or outside in the park.

Sometimes Nathan had to leave for a few days and Misha stayed at his friend's house. That was ok, but it was always the best when Nathan came back and took her home.

But one day, everything felt different.
Nathan packed his going away bag.
Misha didn't like that bag.
It made her tummy hurt.
Still, Nathan always
came back to her.

11

Nathan took Misha to stay with Katrina. ... Katrina was very nice and her apartment had some interesting smells. But Misha hoped that Nathan wouldn't be gone too long.

The next morning, Misha woke up and knew
something was wrong. Katrina seemed worried.
She didn't want play time. Then she started
packing a going away bag! Misha was confused.

That night the Boom Bangs began.
Misha had never heard such
scary sounds, worse than
during thunderstorms.
Misha missed Nathan.

14

The next day, Katrina took Misha
to stay with a man with bushy, black hair.
Misha didn't know him. What was going on?
When was Nathan coming back to get her?
Where did Katrina go?

The man was nice, but he wasn't Nathan.
Misha wanted to go home. But the scary Boom
Bangs kept happening.

16

Misha didn't want to go to the park. The Boom Bangs were louder outdoors.

Still, Misha had to go outside!
The man promised they would go on a quick walk with a few sniffs and come right back home.

At the park, things seemed almost the same.
Misha sniffed around to see
if any friends had been there.

18

Then the Boom Bangs started again!
Misha was so scared she started running.
She ran and ran. She ran until she didn't hear
the Boom Bangs any more.
When she stopped and looked around ...
she was all alone!

Misha sat down under a tree.
What should I do?
How will I find the man
with the black hair?
How will I know when
Nathan gets back?

Nathan! That's what I will do!
I will go home and wait for Nathan!

But Misha had no idea how to find her way home.
She looked around and sniffed, but everything
seemed different.

She walked for a long time. She was very tired.
She came to a nice park and decided to take a nap.
Misha didn't know was that Nathan had asked
other people to help him find her.

23

Misha met a nice man in the park
who and recognised her from photos Nathan posted.
He took Misha to shelter where she waited.

But no Nathan.

24

A lady took picked up Misha at the shelter and
they went to a new house.
At Lana's house, Misha met a cat, Leo,
and a few other dogs.

Still no Nathan.

Lana took Misha and the other animals
on a long car ride. They met a nice couple,
Wendy and Joaiqin, but Nathan wasn't there.

26

Misha wondered if she would ever see Nathan again.
Wendy and Joaqin took Misha on another long ride,
all the way to Bulgaria!

Misha felt happier there.
There were no loud scary noises.
She met a new friend named Sofia.
They had a lot of fun playing together,
but she still missed Nathan. A LOT.

28

One day, Misha heard Nathan's voice.
She looked everywhere, but couldn't find him anywhere.
Then she found his voice coming out of a box screen.

29

Misha and Sofia took another long car ride.
Mischa thought they might be
going to a park to play.

30

Then she heard something! It sounded like Nathan!
Was he in the screen again??? No! He was here!
Right in front of her! She was so happy!
And so was Nathan!

Nathan promised Misha that he would not leave her
alone again. This time they would take a long trip
together. But they weren't going back to Kyiv.
They were going to a new,
safer place called Argentina.
Thank you, Sofia. Goodbye!

Argentina was far away from Kyiv.
But Misha was happy. She got a new bed
and a new bowl and a few new toys.
Most important,
she could hang out with Nathan again.

THE END!